BASEBALL
FOR KIDS

D1445468

BASEBALL
FOR KIDS

A YOUNG FAN'S GUIDE TO
THE HISTORY OF THE GAME

ADAM C. MACKINNON

ROCKRIDGE
PRESS

FOR MEG AND VIOLET,
MY ALL-STAR TEAM

CONTENTS

WELCOME TO THE HISTORY OF BASEBALL!

April's just the best, isn't it? The weather is starting to warm up a little bit, the grass is green, and it's the start of baseball season. My name is Adam, and I'm a baseball writer. I've been a baseball fan as long as I can remember, and my favorite team is the Atlanta Braves. Part of my job is to tell stories about baseball, and I'd like to tell you my own first baseball story. When I was about six or seven years old, my dad took me to my first Major League game. The Braves were playing the Philadelphia Phillies that day at Veterans Stadium in Philadelphia, and it was chilly. I remember the stadium being HUGE, and the field was so GREEN! The air smelled like peanuts and hot dogs, and I loved it. The Braves lost that day, but I didn't care—I got to see it in person!

Baseball has been called one of America's greatest inventions, even though no one really knows how it started. Even if you've never been to a baseball game, you may have heard the famous song "Take Me Out to the Ball Game" or, after you've done a good job, been told that you're "on the ball." These are examples of ways that baseball has become a part of our daily lives. Maybe you've heard a phrase that came from baseball and didn't even know it!

This book is filled with fun facts, interesting trivia, and cool stories that will hopefully help you better understand baseball and all of its history. There are important stories to tell, like ones about Babe Ruth, who was called the "Great Bambino." Or maybe the one about Jackie Robinson. Jackie was the first African American to play organized modern baseball and later became a leader in the Civil Rights Movement. Baseball has been part of our country for more than 100 years and has become as American as apple pie and blue jeans.

There may be some words and phrases that you do not understand right away, but that's okay! Check out the glossary at the end of the book (page 75). If that doesn't work, then ask your parents or even watch a baseball game. Until then, read on and

PLAY BALL!

RISE OF THE MAJOR LEAGUES

The truth is, baseball doesn't have a true beginning. Early on, some people called it "Town Ball," while others just called it "Base." There weren't a lot of rules, and there wasn't any way to keep score. There wasn't really a way to decide on winners—sometimes games would go on for days! Over time, the games became more organized, and eventually, the first professional teams were formed.

THE NEW YORK KNICKERBOCKERS

The New York Knickerbockers in 1858

Alexander Cartwright wasn't always a baseball person. In fact, he worked in a bank. But he liked to play bat and ball games. In the early 1840s, he and his friends got together and formed the first ever professional baseball team. They called themselves the New York Knickerbocker Base Ball Club.

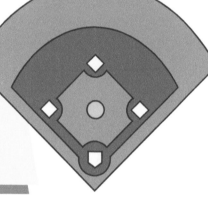

The teams played according to the Knickerbocker Rules. These included the invention of the STRIKEOUT, the foul ball, and batting order. They also said that bases should be equally spaced in a diamond shape.

Even though the team was from New York, they couldn't find enough space in the city. So, they played their home games across the Hudson River in HOBOKEN, NEW JERSEY.

The Knickerbockers hosted a team called the NEW YORK NINE for the first ever organized baseball game. They lost 23–1, which was a really bad game for the Knickerbockers!

THE FIRST PROFESSIONAL TEAMS

Following the Knickerbockers' example, other teams began to form in cities and towns across the country. Teams didn't pay their players, and they were made up of normal townspeople. That changed in 1869 with the Cincinnati Red Stockings. They were the first team entirely made up of paid, professional players.

Though the RED STOCKINGS played their home games in Cincinnati, only one player from the city was on the roster.

The Cincinnati Red Stockings in 1868

The team won its first 81 games in a row, an amazing record that still stands today!

After they lost game number 82, the team broke up just 16 games later.

THE FIRST PROFESSIONAL LEAGUES

The National Baseball Commission helped organize the leagues

The Red Stockings inspired other cities to create their own professional baseball teams. But now, there were so many teams that they had a hard time organizing the games. They needed a good way to set schedules, decide how much to charge for tickets, and make sure that no one was cheating.

The NATIONAL LEAGUE was formed in 1876, mostly because teams didn't always play by the rules if they didn't want to.

In 1901, the AMERICAN LEAGUE was formed to compete with the National League. They offered benefits to fans, like cheaper tickets and games on Sunday!

Both leagues only allowed white men to play, shutting out AFRICAN AMERICANS, LATINOS, and WOMEN from playing organized baseball.

THE FIRST WORLD SERIES

For many years, the National and American Leagues fought with each other over who could attract the best players and teams. To help make things better, they agreed to match up the winners of their leagues to face off against each other. In 1903, the first contest featured the Boston Americans from the American League and the Pittsburgh Pirates representing the National League. They called it the "World's Series."

The first World Series in 1903

It was decided that the teams would play a "BEST OF NINE" series, which means the first team to win five games was the winner.

The crowds in PITTSBURGH were so huge that they spilled into the outfield. If a player hit the ball into the crowd, it was an automatic triple.

BOSTON won the last four games in a row, using only three pitchers (CY YOUNG, BILL DINNEEN, and TOM HUGHES) to beat the Pirates and win the series.

CY YOUNG

Cy Young throwing a baseball in 1908

In 1890, a 23-year-old man named Denton "Cy" Young started his first career game in the Major Leagues. He would go on to start 814 more and become one of the most important pitchers in baseball history. He set records that still stand after over 100 years.

Cy Young holds the ALL-TIME RECORD for wins, with 511. No one else has ever even come close!

He pitched more than 7,300 innings in his career. Only one other pitcher in history has ever pitched over 6,000.

DID YOU KNOW?
Every year, the best pitcher in each league is given the CY YOUNG AWARD in his honor.

THE DEAD BALL ERA

Between the years 1900 and 1919, scoring runs in professional baseball was not an easy thing to do. Hitters would typically advance just one base at a time because they couldn't hit the ball out of the park!

In this era, many pitchers would scuff the baseball with sandpaper, bottle caps, or even nails! Sometimes they would cover it with dirt or mud or saliva and call it a "SPIT BALL."

A batter takes a swing in the Dead Ball Era

BASE RUNNERS would steal bases a lot as a way to move up a base when the pitcher wasn't looking!

STELLAR STAT:
In 1902, Socks Seybold set the record for the most home runs in a season with 16.
In 2019, 162 players hit more than 16 home runs.

THE CHICAGO "BLACK SOX" OF 1919

Edward Victor Cicotte, a player for the Chicago White Sox, throwing a baseball

During the Dead Ball Era, baseball had a problem with gambling. Gambling is when you risk money in a game or a bet and you hope to win a prize or money. In the 1919 World Series, the Chicago White Sox had a much better lineup and pitching, but they lost to the Cincinnati Reds. Everyone was surprised. Later, people found out the White Sox had cheated and lost on purpose!

It became known as the "Black Sox" team because its cheating left a BLACK MARK on baseball.

Many people say that outfielder "SHOELESS" Joe Jackson would be in the Baseball Hall of Fame if he hadn't taken part.

Q&A: So what happened to the eight players who cheated?

Answer: They were banned for life from organized baseball and not allowed into the Hall of Fame.

2

THE HOME RUN ERA

Up until this point, baseball rules really favored the pitcher. A lot of times, games were low scoring and didn't show off the star players. Baseball needed a way to increase the number of runs scored so fans would come to the ballpark and watch the games. The leagues made changes that brought in a new era of baseball, closer to the kind of game we see today.

THE END OF THE DEAD BALL ERA

Babe Ruth taking a swing

In the early days, many games were played with only a couple baseballs. The balls would start out white and round. As the games went on, the balls would turn brown and change shape. They became very hard for batters to see. In the 1920s, the umpires started replacing the dirty, used balls with clean, new ones.

In 1920, the MAJOR LEAGUES outlawed the spit ball. Now pitchers couldn't scratch, spit on, or change the ball in any way to make it dip, dive, or sink in midair.

Any ball that was DISCOLORED or MISSHAPEN was replaced with a brand-new WHITE BASEBALL that was more visible to hitters.

The average number of runs per game increased from 3.88 runs per game in 1919 to 5.13 runs per game by 1925.

BABE RUTH

There probably hasn't been a more important player in the history of baseball than George Herman Ruth. They called him "Babe" because of his baby-like appearance despite his broad shoulders and barrel-like chest. He was best known for hitting huge home runs and having a great time while doing it.

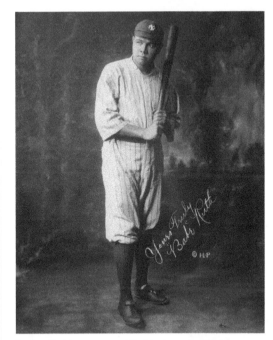
Babe Ruth poses with his baseball bat

Ruth was born in BALTIMORE and had a hard life as a child. He learned to play baseball in boarding school. In 1914, he started his career as a pitcher with the BOSTON RED SOX.

Many people know he set records for hitting. But he was also an EXCELLENT PITCHER.

STELLAR STAT:
Ruth once pitched
29 consecutive innings in the
WORLD SERIES
without letting
the other team score.
That record stood
for 43 years.

THE NEGRO LEAGUES

The Pittsburgh Crawfords of the Negro Leagues in 1935

For African American men who wanted to play baseball, the Major Leagues weren't a welcoming place. In the 1920s, they were still banned from competing. So, they decided to form their own league. The Negro Leagues played a different, faster style than the Majors and were just as good.

The KANSAS CITY MONARCHS and HOMESTEAD GRAYS from Pittsburgh were the most dominant teams in the league.

Unfortunately, stats weren't always kept at these games. A lot of records aren't totally accurate or remain a mystery, like the number of games SATCHEL PAIGE actually pitched.

TRUE/FALSE: Many Negro League teams didn't have a home field and would play in Major League parks when that team was away.

Answer: True!

JOSH GIBSON

Of all the players in the Negro Leagues, Josh Gibson may be the most legendary. He was a power-hitting catcher, and he played for the Pittsburgh Crawfords and the Homestead Grays. He died at a young age, but stories of his amazing hitting are still told to this day.

Josh Gibson of the Pittsburgh Crawfords

No one really knows how many home runs Gibson hit, but many estimate it was more than 800 or maybe even closer to 1,000. This would be the most of any player EVER!

The most famous Gibson home run tale says he hit the ball completely out of the old YANKEE STADIUM, a feat even BABE RUTH couldn't match.

DID YOU KNOW?

One story said that Gibson hit a home run out of sight in Pittsburgh. The next day, he was playing in Philadelphia when a ball fell from the sky and was caught by an out-fielder. The umpire yelled, "YOU'RE OUT! YESTERDAY!"

LOU GEHRIG

Lou Gehrig (left) and Babe Ruth (right)

Baseball is a tough sport. Even the best players need a day off. Lou Gehrig was different. No aches or pains kept him out of the lineup. Plus he was a great player. Sadly, his career was cut short by a life-threatening disease called ALS. The disease became known as Lou Gehrig's disease in his honor.

Gehrig earned his nickname "THE IRON HORSE" for his durability. He played in a record 2,130 games in a row.

He won two MOST VALUABLE PLAYER AWARDS in his career and led the league in home runs three times between 1931 and 1936.

WHO SAID IT?: "HE WAS THERE DAY AFTER DAY AND YEAR AFTER YEAR. HE NEVER SULKED OR WHINED . . ." —SPORTSWRITER JOHN KIERAN IN THE NEW YORK TIMES

YANKEE DOMINANCE

The Yankees became the best team in the Major Leagues between 1920 and 1940. They went to the World Series 11 times and won it eight times. Besides Babe Ruth and Lou Gehrig, the Yankees had many other great players.

The New York Yankees in 1927

From the 1920s through the 1940s, they faced the NEW YORK GIANTS five times in the World Series and went 3–2 against them.

The most famous of those teams were the 1927 Yankees. Their feared lineup was called "MURDERERS' ROW." They earned that name because they were so hard on pitchers that they would "murder" baseballs!

STELLAR STAT: The YANKEES WON four World Series in a row from 1936 to 1939. No other team in history has ever done that besides . . . the Yankees in the 1950s.

CONNIE MACK

Connie Mack, on the left, in 1911

Cornelius McGillicuddy was a catcher for the Pittsburgh Pirates in the late 1800s. In 1901, he became the manager of the Philadelphia Athletics. He shortened his name to Connie Mack so it would fit on the scorecards he would give to umpires. He would become the greatest manager of all time.

In 1953, Philadelphia renamed SHIBE PARK, where the A's had played since 1909, Connie Mack Stadium.

He went to the World Series nine times in his career and won it five times. In 1929, his A's staged the greatest comeback in World Series history, scoring 10 runs in one inning! That inning was called "THE MACK ATTACK."

STELLAR STAT:
Mack holds the
ALL-TIME RECORD
for games won as a
manager, with
3,731.

3

BREAKING BARRIERS

In the 1940s, a lot of change was happening in the world, and baseball was changing with it. World War II forced some of baseball's best players to leave the field and join the military. Women and African Americans would finally find a place to play on the field. It was a time when the game needed to adapt, and it gave us some of baseball's most memorable characters.

WORLD WAR II AND BASEBALL

Ted Williams in 1952

When the United States joined World War II, many of baseball's best and brightest stars were drafted to join the military. President Franklin Roosevelt said that baseball should continue to be played. Americans were working hard and needed something fun to help them relax. This made owners get creative in finding players.

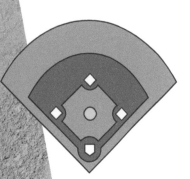

TED WILLIAMS, who many thought was the best hitter who ever lived, left baseball twice to fly for the AIR FORCE.

The baseball season and WORLD SERIES were held every year during the war. Teams sometimes used replacement players or brought back players from retirement.

TRUE/FALSE: Though they weren't excused, not many baseball players went to war.

Answer: False! Five hundred Major Leaguers and 2,000 Minor League players were drafted.

SATCHEL PAIGE

Satchel Paige was a star pitcher in the Negro Leagues. He played for many different teams all across the country. Paige eventually joined the Major Leagues in 1948 and played for the Cleveland Indians.

No one really knew how old Satchel was until he joined the INDIANS. They found out he was 42 years old.

Satchel Paige of the Cleveland Indians in 1949

Paige was voted into the HALL OF FAME in 1971. He only played 176 games in the Major Leagues, which is the least of any pitcher currently in the Hall.

STELLAR STAT:
Paige holds the all-time record for OLDEST PLAYER to pitch in a Major League game. He was almost 60 years old when he pitched one game for the then-named KANSAS CITY ATHLETICS.

THE ALL-AMERICAN GIRLS PROFESSIONAL BASEBALL LEAGUE

Players of the Kenosha Comets, an AAGPBL team, in 1943

In 1943, many of baseball's players were off to fight in World War II. Some people were worried that fans would lose interest in professional baseball. So, a few team owners came up with a separate league made up of women. It was called the All-American Girls Professional Baseball League (AAGPBL). It was the first time women would play professional baseball.

By the time the league ended in 1954, over ONE MILLION fans had paid to see AAGPBL games!

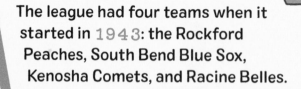

The league had four teams when it started in 1943: the Rockford Peaches, South Bend Blue Sox, Kenosha Comets, and Racine Belles.

WHO SAID IT?: "THE LEAGUE WAS EXTREMELY COMPETITIVE, AND MORE SO AS THE YEARS WENT BY. THE TOUGHER IT GOT, THE MORE I LIKED IT."
—JEAN FAUT, AAGPBL PITCHER

JOE DIMAGGIO

Joe DiMaggio played outfield for the New York Yankees. He is one of the most famous players in baseball history, even though he was a very quiet person. He is known for setting the record for longest hitting streak in baseball history: 56 games in a row with a hit! No one has ever come close to it since, and many call the record unbreakable.

DiMaggio was voted to the ALL-STAR team every season he played, a total of 13 times. He also won the MOST VALUABLE PLAYER AWARD three times.

JOE DI MAGGIO
Salutes His Bat

© 1941.. *The Sporting News Pub. Co.*

Joe DiMaggio kissing his bat

STELLAR STAT:
DiMaggio led the American League in home runs twice (1937 and 1948) and batting average twice (1939 and 1940).

In 1941, jazz musician LES BROWN wrote the song "JOLTIN' JOE DIMAGGIO" after DiMaggio's hitting streak that season, and it turned out to be a hit!

TED WILLIAMS

Ted Williams takes a swing in 1952

Ted Williams was an outfielder for the Boston Red Sox during the 1940s and 1950s. He was one of the players who went to war during his playing time, and he received medals for his service. Many think he is the greatest hitter who ever lived.

He hit 521 home runs in his career. That puts him in the all-time top 20 leaders.

STELLAR STAT:
Williams led the league in home runs
FOUR TIMES,
and he scored the most runs
SIX TIMES.

He's one of only two players ever to win the TRIPLE CROWN AWARD TWICE (which means he led the league in home runs, runs batted in, and batting average).

JACKIE ROBINSON: BREAKING THE COLOR BARRIER

When Jackie Robinson took the field on April 15, 1947, with the Brooklyn Dodgers, many considered it the biggest day in baseball. Before that day, not a single African American had put on a Major League uniform. He was given a very hard time by both the players and the fans, but he didn't fight back. Instead, he rose above and became a very important person in baseball history.

Jackie Robinson pitching

He was elected to the
HALL OF FAME in 1962.

Robinson was selected for the ALL-STAR team six times. He won the ROOKIE OF THE YEAR AWARD during his first season and the Most Valuable Player award in 1949.

DID YOU KNOW?

His uniform number, 42, is the only number that has been retired by ALL MAJOR LEAGUE CLUBS. This means that, in his honor, NO ONE can wear that number.

THE END OF THE NEGRO LEAGUES

Souvenir coins depicting players from the 1960s and 1970s

When Jackie Robinson opened the door for other African American players, everyone knew it was just a matter of time before others walked through it. This was a great thing for the country and for Major League baseball. It also meant that the Negro Leagues would likely end.

Branch Rickey, the general manager who signed JACKIE ROBINSON to a Major League contract, signed other Negro League players shortly after. These included pitcher DON NEWCOMBE and catcher ROY CAMPANELLA.

Even though the LAST NEGRO ALL-STAR GAME was played in 1962, the Indianapolis Clowns continued to play exhibition games all the way into the 1980s.

TRUE/FALSE: Hank Aaron was the last active player in the Major Leagues who also played in the Negro Leagues.

Answer: True!

4

BASEBALL MOVES WEST

In the 1950s, New York City was dominating the baseball scene. The Giants, Dodgers, and Yankees won their leagues almost every year and had some of the greatest players in the game. By the end of the 1950s, two of those teams would follow many of their fans out to California. Soon, teams were popping up all over the country, from Georgia to Texas and Minnesota to California. The country was on the move, and baseball was going with it.

NEW YORK DOMINATION

1951 World Series game three in New York City

For many, New York City was considered the capital of baseball. The Yankees, Dodgers, and Giants were all very good teams and had more star players than anyone else. The teams had big stadiums in the city. The stands would fill up with neighbors, friends, and family members, all rooting for different teams!

The Yankees were the best of the three teams, WINNING FIVE WORLD SERIES in a row from 1949 to 1953.

At one point, Joe DiMaggio (Yankees), Willie Mays (Giants), Jackie Robinson (Dodgers), Mickey Mantle (Yankees), Duke Snider (Dodgers), and many other HALL OF FAME PLAYERS were all playing in NEW YORK at the same time.

STELLAR STAT:
A New York team made it to the World Series 10 times in a row between 1949 and 1958. Six of those times, both sides were from NEW YORK.

WILLIE MAYS

In 1951, the New York Giants signed a talented young outfielder from the Birmingham Black Barons, a Negro League team. That outfielder was Willie Mays. Nicknamed "The Say Hey Kid," Mays would go on to be one of the greatest players in baseball history.

He won the GOLD GLOVE AWARD (given to the best fielder at each position) 12 times in a row, the SECOND-LONGEST STREAK in baseball history.

Willie Mays holding his baseball bat

STELLAR STAT: In his career, Mays hit 660 home runs, stole 338 bases, and finished with 3,283 hits.

He's one of only three players ever with more than 600 home runs and 300 stolen bases. The other two are ALEX RODRIGUEZ and MAYS'S godson, BARRY BONDS.

THE SHOT HEARD 'ROUND THE WORLD

People watching the 1951 World Series on television

In 1951, the New York Giants and the Brooklyn Dodgers finished the regular season tied with each other. They played a three-game series to decide who would go on to play the Yankees in the World Series. The Giants won the first game, and then the Dodgers won the second. In the third game, the Dodgers were winning by two runs until the ninth inning, when Bobby Thompson hit a three-run home run off Ralph Branca. The Giants had won the pennant!

It was called "The Shot Heard 'Round the Baseball World" by the *NEW YORK DAILY NEWS* because it was televised and MILLIONS were watching.

The GIANTS would end up losing to the YANKEES in the World Series that season.

WHO SAID IT?: "THE GIANTS WIN THE PENNANT! THE GIANTS WIN THE PENNANT!" —BROADCASTER RUSS HODGES, CALLING THE HOME RUN FROM THE RADIO BOOTH

THE FIRST TELEVISED GAMES

Watching baseball on television is a part of American life. Before the 1950s, however, the only way to enjoy a baseball game was to either go the park or listen on the radio. Television brought the games to the rest of the country, so fans could see their heroes, even from far away.

A television camera in a ballpark

The first baseball game on TV was between the CINCINNATI REDS and the BROOKLYN DODGERS during the 1939 World's Fair.

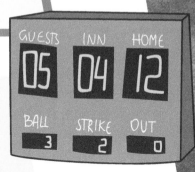

In 1988, more than 130 million people watched the World Series between the LOS ANGELES DODGERS and OAKLAND ATHLETICS.

WHO SAID IT?: "UNBELIEVABLE! A HOME RUN FOR GIBSON! AND THE DODGERS HAVE WON THE GAME, 5-4! I DON'T BELIEVE WHAT I JUST SAW!" —BROADCASTER JACK BUCK, CALLING KIRK GIBSON'S GAME-WINNING HOME RUN IN THE FIRST GAME OF THE 1988 WORLD SERIES

THE MAJOR LEAGUES MOVE WEST

San Francisco Giants welcome parade in 1958

In the late 1950s, a lot of Americans wanted to escape the hustle and bustle of the big cities like New York and Boston. So, they started to move out West. In 1957, it was clear that New York could no longer support three baseball teams at the same time. As attendance began to go down, the teams began to leave.

In 1958, the BROOKLYN DODGERS moved to LOS ANGELES. For the first time since 1884, professional baseball would not be played in BROOKLYN.

The NEW YORK GIANTS joined the DODGERS in moving to California and settled in SAN FRANCISCO.

TRUE/FALSE: New York never added another baseball team after the Giants and Dodgers left.

Answer: False! The New York Mets came along in 1962.

THE GAME CONTINUES TO GROW

When the 1960 season finished, there were 16 Major League teams. Since then, the league has almost doubled, now hosting 30 teams. These days, fans in places like Minnesota, Colorado, Arizona, and Washington have a home team they can root for.

A young boy hoping to catch a fly ball

In 1961, the FIRST TEAMS to join the MAJOR LEAGUES were the Los Angeles Angels, Minnesota Twins, Washington Senators, New York Mets, and Houston Colt .45s.

In 1969, four more teams were added: the Kansas City Royals, San Diego Padres, Montreal Expos, and Seattle Pilots. There were now 24 teams.

In the 1990s, the Colorado Rockies, Tampa Bay Devil Rays, Arizona Diamondbacks, and Florida Marlins eventually brought us to the 30 teams we have today.

FRANK ROBINSON

Frank Robinson in his Cincinnati Reds uniform

When Frank Robinson came into the big leagues in 1956, everyone knew he was a great player. What people didn't know was that he would go on to become one of the best players of all time. He even made history after he retired as a player.

Q&A: How many home runs did Frank Robinson hit?

Answer: He hit 586 home runs in his career, the 10th most of all time.

When he was named the manager of the 1975 Cleveland Indians, he became the FIRST AFRICAN AMERICAN MANAGER in baseball history.

Robinson is the only player in baseball history to win the MOST VALUABLE PLAYER AWARD in both the American and National Leagues.

5

BREAKING RECORDS

As interest in baseball continued to grow across the country, the game continued to change. There were some small changes to the field that brought on an era of great pitchers. But it was a power hitter who broke a record many thought would never be broken. Some teams saw good times, and some saw bad times, but one team managed to see both. New star players made their debuts, and sadly, one was lost too soon.

NEW FACES IN NEW PLACES

Rod Carew of the Minnesota Twins in 1969

As baseball expanded to the rest of the country, new players began to make names for themselves. Teams were in need of players now, and more people got a shot to play in the big leagues. These players didn't miss their chance.

DID YOU KNOW?

Reggie Jackson of the Oakland Athletics hit 563 home runs. He got the nickname "MR. OCTOBER" for his great performances in the playoffs. He was elected into the Hall of Fame in 1993.

Tom Seaver of the New York Mets won 311 games. He won three CY YOUNG AWARDS. He was elected into the Hall of Fame in 1992.

ROD CAREW of the Minnesota Twins led the league in batting average seven times and had over 3,000 hits. He was elected into the Hall of Fame in 1991.

PITCHING DOMINANCE

For many years since Babe Ruth, the game had always been about the batter. Suddenly, in the mid-1960s, the pitchers took control. Batting averages dropped, and home runs were much less common. Many called this the Second Dead Ball Era.

Bob Gibson of the St. Louis Cardinals

In 1968, Hall of Fame pitcher BOB GIBSON had one of the best seasons ever recorded. He allowed just over one run per game, and he struck out 268 batters.

SANDY KOUFAX struck out 382 batters in 1965, the most in a season since 1884.

Q&A: Why did pitchers do so well during this time?

Answer: Many say that it's because the pitcher's mound was raised up, which made the ball harder for batters to see.

THE MIRACLE METS

The New York Mets celebrating a win in 1969

When the New York Mets finished their first season in 1962, they posted the worst record in the history of baseball: 40 wins and 120 losses. They were the joke of the Major Leagues for a little while, until 1969 when a magical event occurred: The Mets learned how to win.

During their miracle season, the Mets won 100 games. They also beat their rivals, the Atlanta Braves, to win the NATIONAL LEAGUE PENNANT.

Thanks to amazing catches from outfielders TOMMIE AGEE and RON SWOBODA, they beat the Baltimore Orioles in the World Series in five games.

The Mets star pitcher TOM SEAVER won the CY YOUNG AWARD that season, winning 25 games that year.

HANK AARON

Henry Louis Aaron was a quiet, mild-mannered young man who could hit a baseball very hard and very far. He was signed by the Boston Braves in 1952. He stayed with the team even after they moved to Milwaukee and later to Atlanta. He ended up being one of the best home run hitters in baseball history.

Hank Aaron holding baseball bats

STELLAR STAT:
Aaron still holds the all-time record—2,297—for times he scored his teammates. These are called RUNS BATTED IN, or RBIs for short.

Despite hitting so many home runs over his career, he never hit more than 44 in a SINGLE SEASON.

Aaron hit 755 home runs in his career, passing Babe Ruth and holding the ALL-TIME RECORD until Barry Bonds broke it in 2007.

THE BIG RED MACHINE

The Cincinnati Reds in the 1970s

In the 1970s, the scariest opponent a team could see on their schedule was the Cincinnati Reds. They had the toughest lineup in baseball and a pretty good pitching staff. Between 1970 and 1979, the Reds won the National League pennant four times and the World Series twice. Many historians say they were the best team in baseball history!

TRUE/FALSE: The Big Red Machine produced three Hall of Fame players and one Hall of Fame manager.

Answer: True! Joe Morgan, Tony Pérez, Johnny Bench, and manager Sparky Anderson were all voted into the Hall!

They won back-to-back WORLD SERIES in 1974 and 1975. This hadn't been done in over 50 years.

STELLAR STAT: If you add up all the Reds players awards during those years, you get 63 All-Star appearances, 25 GOLD GLOVE AWARDS, and 6 MOST VALUABLE PLAYER AWARDS.

ROBERTO CLEMENTE

Roberto Clemente was a Puerto Rican outfielder who played for the Pittsburgh Pirates. He was a great player as well as a humanitarian. He often gave back to his native country. In 1972, while flying to Puerto Rico to help earthquake victims, his plane crashed, and he was killed.

Roberto Clemente statue in Pittsburgh, PA

Clemente collected exactly 3,000 hits in his career. Over his career, he led the league in batting average FOUR TIMES.

He threw out 254 BASE RUNNERS from the outfield, the second most in the history of baseball.

Every year, baseball gives out an award in his name to the most CHARITABLE BASEBALL PLAYER of that season. He was elected to the Hall of Fame in 1973, after a special election.

SANDY KOUFAX

Sandy Koufax of the Los Angeles Dodgers

When Sandy Koufax joined the Brooklyn Dodgers in 1955, he could throw the ball very hard. The problem was he didn't exactly know where it was going. After a few years, he figured out how to throw more accurately. That earned him a Hall of Fame career that lasted just 11 seasons.

He is the YOUNGEST PERSON ever elected to the Hall of Fame.

Koufax led the National League in STRIKEOUTS FOUR TIMES in his career and had a total of 2,396.

He pitched FOUR NO HITTERS, the second most ever of any Major League pitcher. One of those was a PERFECT GAME. A perfect game is when no opposing batter reaches base.

6

BASEBALL TODAY

It has been over 120 years since the first baseball games were played. Good teams like the New York Yankees and St. Louis Cardinals continued to win. And two teams that had failed to win for around 100 years finally won a title and broke ancient "curses" that haunted their fans. Also, home runs became so common that records were being broken all the time. The game continues to be exciting and fun for fans of all ages, and that is one thing that has never changed.

BASE STEALING

Rickey Henderson stealing a base in 1983

Stealing bases was pretty common in the early days of baseball, during the Dead Ball Era. Back then, the ball would rarely get past the outfielders. Batters were forced to try to advance one base at a time. In modern times, stealing a base is a strategy to force pitchers to throw harder and tire out faster.

In 1920, at the end of the DEAD BALL ERA, players stole 990 bases. In 2011, there were 3,279 bases stolen!

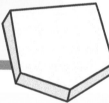

The last player to steal 100 bases in a season was ST. LOUIS CARDINALS outfielder Vince Coleman in 1987.

STELLAR STAT:
Oakland A's outfielder RICKEY HENDERSON holds the all-time record for stolen bases. He stole 1,406 bases over his career through the 1980s and '90s.

RELIEF PITCHING

In the early days of baseball, the pitcher who started a game usually finished it. Managers didn't like to pull their starter unless things were pretty bad. Now, it's rare for a starting pitcher to finish a game. Managers will sometimes use five relievers or more in a game.

Mariano Rivera of the New York Yankees in the 2000s

STELLAR STAT:
MARIANO RIVERA **is thought of as the best reliever of all time. He recorded 652 saves, the most by any pitcher.**

Q&A: What is a "save"?

Answer: In 1969, the "save" was a stat created for pitchers who came in to close games and help their team win. This created the "closer" role.

In 1948 and 1949, 24 different pitchers threw at least 16 complete games (where the starting pitcher throws the whole game). In 2018 and 2019, no one threw more than THREE GAMES.

HOME RUN MANIA!

Mark McGwire of the St. Louis Cardinals hits a home run

In 1998, Sammy Sosa of the Chicago Cubs and Mark McGwire of the St. Louis Cardinals began a home run race that became national news. Why were players hitting home runs more often than ever before? There were rumors at the time that some players were cheating to get bigger and stronger. Either way, the fans loved it.

MCGWIRE ultimately won the race. He finished with 70 home runs that season. SAMMY SOSA finished with 66.

In 1986, baseball players hit 3,813 home runs. That was a record number. In 2019, they hit 6,776 home runs, the most ever.

WHO SAID IT?: "I THREW A NINETY-SEVEN MILE PER HOUR PITCH TO [MARK] MCGWIRE, AND IT WENT OUT AT A HUNDRED AND TEN!" —HALL OF FAME PITCHER RANDY JOHNSON

THE YANKEES RETURN

In the 1996 World Series, the New York Yankees faced the Atlanta Braves. The Yankees lost the first two games, but they came back and won the next four in a row to win the championship. This was their first title in 18 years. They went to the World Series five more times in a row and won three of them. The Yankees of the 1990s are remembered as one of the greatest teams of all time.

The New York Yankees in the 1990s

DID YOU KNOW?
The two series that they lost were to the FLORIDA MARLINS in 1997 and the ARIZONA DIAMONDBACKS in 2001.

When it was over, the YANKEES had won their 23rd, 24th, 25th, and 26th WORLD SERIES titles.

MARIANO RIVERA, DEREK JETER, JORGE POSADA, and ROGER CLEMENS were the stars of the team during those years.

THE RED SOX AND CUBS BREAK THEIR CURSES

A bronze lion wearing a Cubs cap to celebrate the Chicago Cubs' first World Series Championship in 108 years

Boston Red Sox fans have known much sadness when it comes to their team. In 2004, they hadn't won a World Series title in 86 years. Fans of the Chicago Cubs had to wait over 100 years for their World Series title in 2016! Many fans believed that both teams were cursed. But both teams broke through eventually!

When the Red Sox beat the St. Louis Cardinals in 2004, they say they broke the CURSE OF THE BAMBINO. The curse started when they traded Babe Ruth to the Yankees in 1919.

The Chicago Cubs beat the Cleveland Indians in 2016 to break the CURSE OF THE BILLY GOAT. That curse started in 1945 when a fan was asked to remove his billy goat from Wrigley Field.

DID YOU KNOW?
The car, airplane, telephone, and television were all invented in between the years when the RED SOX and the CUBS won WORLD SERIES titles.

BREAKING RECORDS

In the 1990s and beyond, many records were broken. Stolen bases, saves, career games, and, of course, many records related to home runs. While some broken records were said to be unfair, some were celebrated across the country. After all, records are made to be broken!

Ichiro Suzuki of the Seattle Mariners in 2009

Barry Bonds of the San Francisco Giants passed Hank Aaron as the ALL-TIME HOME RUN LEADER. He finished with 762.

STELLAR STAT:
In 1995, Cal Ripken Jr. played in his 2,131st consecutive game for the BALTIMORE ORIOLES. This broke Lou Gehrig's (page 14) previous record.

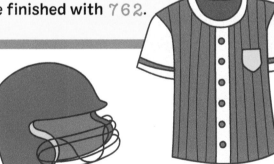

In 2004, Seattle Mariners outfielder ICHIRO SUZUKI set the all-time record for hits in a single season. He collected 262, breaking St. Louis Browns first baseman GEORGE SISLER'S record set in 1920.

FUTURE STARS

Little League World Series in 2019

Baseball is a game about the future as well as the past. One day, the records that were set by players we've talked about in this book will be broken. In many ways, the game will always change as we get older, but there are parts that will always stay the same. These players show that baseball has a bright future and will continue on for a long time!

MIKE TROUT could break a lot of records in the future! He has already won two Most Valuable Player awards, was named ROOKIE OF THE YEAR, and has hit almost 300 home runs!

CLAYTON KERSHAW could be the greatest pitcher of the last 50 years, winning the CY YOUNG AWARD three times and a Most Valuable Player award. Plus he has over 2,400 strikeouts.

There are many exciting new players in the league today. Some could even be on YOUR HOMETOWN TEAM!

7

MORE FAN-TASTIC TRIVIA

Now you know that baseball is a game with over 120 years of history behind it and a lot more future ahead of it as well! Going to a game or watching it on TV is a fun experience, but it can be even more fun if you know a little more about how it is played! In this chapter, we'll learn about some rules of the game and stellar stats, as well as some interesting trivia about the ol' ball game!

RULES OF THE GAME

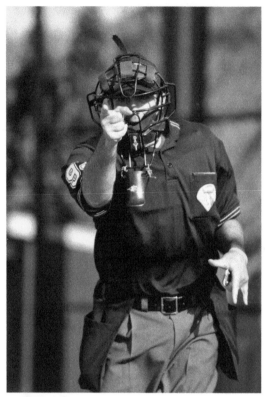

A home plate umpire calls a strike!

Baseball is a game of rules. Some of them are written down, and some of them are not. A lot of them have changed over time to help the game get better, but some have stayed the same since the New York Knickerbockers (page 2) played the first ever professional baseball game in the 1840s.

Q&A: How many umpires are on the field for a game?

Answer: During the regular season, there are four—one at home plate and one at each base. During the playoffs, two more are added, on either side of the outfield.

TRUE/FALSE: If a batter hits the ball in the air and another player catches it in foul territory, the batter is out.

Answer: True!

STELLAR STAT: PETE ROSE made the most outs in baseball history with 10,328.

WHO SAID IT?: "I MADE A GAME EFFORT TO ARGUE, BUT TWO THINGS WERE AGAINST ME: THE UMPIRES AND THE RULES." —HALL OF FAME MANAGER LEO DUROCHER

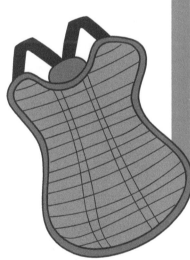

STELLAR STAT: BOBBY COX, **Hall of Fame manager for the** ATLANTA BRAVES, **was thrown out of the game by the umpires 161 times in his career, an all-time record.**

TRUE/FALSE: If the ball and base runner get to the base at the same time, the base runner is out.

Answer: False! The tie goes to the runner.

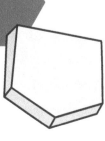

THE UNIFORMS

Classic baseball uniforms

Early on, uniforms were kept simple. They just had the name of the city that the team was from on the front. Players had a number on the back to tell them apart, and each team had its own unique colors. Eventually, team logos and names would replace the cities, and teams now have several different uniforms they can wear. These are called "alternates."

TRUE/FALSE: It has always been a tradition for players to choose their own numbers on the backs of their uniforms.

Answer: False! In the early days, the player's batting order would determine his number.

Q&A: What does it mean when a number is "retired"?

Answer: Having your number retired by your team is considered a great honor. It means that no one who plays for that team can ever wear that number again.

STELLAR STAT:
Starting pitcher EDWIN JACKSON has worn the most different uniforms of any Major League player. He has played for 14 different teams, an all-time record.

STELLAR STAT:

JACKIE ROBINSON
is the only player whose
number (42) is retired
by all Major League
teams.

WHO SAID IT?: "IF MY UNIFORM DOESN'T GET DIRTY, I HAVEN'T DONE ANYTHING IN THE BASEBALL GAME." —HALL OF FAME OUTFIELDER RICKEY HENDERSON

TRUE/FALSE: Teams are allowed to choose which uniform they wear to every game.

Answer: False! There are specific home and away jerseys for each team.

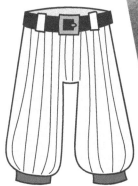

THE CATCHER'S MASKS

Catcher's mask

In the early days of baseball, it was quite a hazard to play catcher. Foul tips, stray pitches, and plays at the plate were often painful experiences. Now, catchers wear protectors for their bodies and a mask for their face.

STELLAR STAT:
The longest streak by a catcher without making an error is 282 games in a row. That record was set by MIKE MATHENY of the ST. LOUIS CARDINALS.

In 1877, JIM TYNG was the first recorded player to wear a catcher's mask while playing for HARVARD UNIVERSITY'S baseball team.

In 1907, New York Giants catcher ROGER BRESNAHAN was the first professional player to wear full protective gear, including a mask, in the Major Leagues.

The most popular version of the modern hockey-style catcher's mask was introduced by TORONTO BLUE JAYS catcher CHARLIE O'BRIEN in 1996.

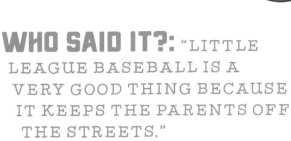

WHO SAID IT?: "LITTLE LEAGUE BASEBALL IS A VERY GOOD THING BECAUSE IT KEEPS THE PARENTS OFF THE STREETS." —HALL OF FAME CATCHER YOGI BERRA

TRUE/FALSE: Today's catcher's masks can weigh more than three pounds.

Answer: True! The modern mask often weighs more than five pounds.

THE GLOVES

Mickey Mantle wearing a baseball glove

The first use of gloves dates back to the 1890s, when Albert Goodwill Spalding encouraged his players to wear them on the field. Before that, players simply played with their bare hands. As pitchers began to throw harder and the ball became harder, players were required to wear gloves in the field to better protect them from injury.

STELLAR STAT: Greg Maddux, a pitcher for the Atlanta Braves, won **18 GOLD GLOVE AWARDS.** That's the most ever by any player, not just a pitcher! The Gold Glove is the award given to the best fielder at each position.

Q&A: How many different types of gloves are there?

Answer: There are four main types of gloves: catcher's mitt (big and pillow-like), first baseman's glove (longer for scooping throws from the dirt), infielder's glove (very small, to get the ball out faster), and outfielder's glove (bigger, with deep pockets for catching fly balls).

WHO SAID IT?: "I USED TO SOAK MY MITTS IN A BUCKET OF WATER FOR ABOUT TWO DAYS. THEN I'D PUT A COUPLE OF BASEBALLS IN THE POCKET AND WRAP IT UP WITH A RUBBER BAND." —BROADCASTER AND FORMER MLB CATCHER BOB UECKER

STELLAR STAT:

There's only ever been one switch thrower in baseball history: PAT VENDITTE. A switch thrower is a pitcher who can pitch with either arm. He uses a special glove that allows him to switch his throwing arm without changing gloves.

TRUE/FALSE: Until 1954, outfielders used to leave their gloves on the field when they went in to bat.

Answer: True! Even though the league changed the rules for fear of players tripping on them, there's no evidence that ever happened.

Q&A: What is a glove made out of?

Answer: Most gloves are made out of heavy leather. They can be stiff when they're brand new. That's why most players spend a lot of time breaking in their gloves when they get new ones.

FAMOUS PITCHES

Sandy Koufax of the Los Angeles Dodgers throws a pitch

As time passed, batters got pretty good at hitting just one kind of pitch. So, pitchers had to figure out ways to make the ball move as it went to the plate. Now, pitchers can make it sink, curve, dive, even dance in the breeze. Some pitchers made their careers on throwing a particular kind of pitch.

TRUE/FALSE: Pitchers are allowed to scratch or scuff the ball to make it spin faster.

Answer: False! Pitchers aren't allowed to modify the ball or rub it with any substance other than rosin, which is out on the pitcher's mound.

STELLAR STAT:
A pitcher named CANDY CUMMINGS invented the curveball in 1867. It was called a "CHEAT" pitch at the time because it was meant to fool batters. Until then, pitchers were expected to just lob the ball so it was easy to hit.

WHO SAID IT?:
"A PITCHER NEEDS TWO PITCHES—ONE THEY'RE LOOKING FOR AND ONE TO CROSS THEM UP."
—HALL OF FAME PITCHER WARREN SPAHN

STELLAR STAT:

In the early 1900s, a pitcher named Eddie Cicotte earned the nickname "KNUCKLES" for his signature knuckleball pitch. A knuckleball doesn't spin when the pitcher throws it. Instead, it wobbles in the breeze. Batters say the ball "DANCES" on the way to the plate.

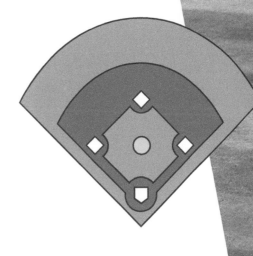

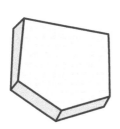

TRUE/FALSE: There aren't any underhand pitchers in baseball.

Answer: False! There are some famous ones, like Chad Bradford of the Oakland A's.

Q&A: How many types of pitches are there?

Answer: There are quite a few, but the most popular ones are the fastball, slider, curveball, changeup, and knuckleball.

GUESTS 05 · INN 04 · HOME 12
BALL 3 · STRIKE 2 · OUT 0

SLUGGERS

Frank Robinson of the Baltimore Orioles swings the bat

A batter who hits the ball with power is called a "slugger." The term is borrowed from boxing. (A slugger is when a boxer throws big, long punches rather than sharp, short ones.) They're sometimes called power hitters, and their main job is to hit lots of home runs.

TRUE/FALSE: The most home runs hit in a single season is 73.

Answer: True! Barry Bonds set the record in 2001.

Q&A: Who hit the longest home run ever?

Answer: In 1921, Babe Ruth hit the longest single home run in Major League history. It traveled 560 feet and sailed clear out of Tiger Stadium in Detroit.

STELLAR STAT:
When Babe Ruth retired with 714 home runs, the next closest to him was ROGER CONNOR. Connor retired in 1897 with 138 home runs.

STELLAR STAT:
BARRY BONDS
holds the all-time record for
home runs in a career.
He hit 762. Some people
feel like he cheated
and say it doesn't
count.

WHO SAID IT?: "SOMEONE ONCE ASKED ME IF I EVER WENT UP TO THE PLATE TRYING TO HIT A HOME RUN. I SAID, 'SURE, EVERY TIME.'" —HALL OF FAME OUTFIELDER MICKEY MANTLE

TRUE/FALSE: A home run doesn't count if it doesn't leave the field.

Answer: False! There is such a thing as an inside-the-park home run.

FAMOUS BALLPARKS

The Pittsburgh Pirates' Major League Baseball stadium in Pennsylvania

As long as there has been professional baseball, there have been professional ballparks. Sometimes they're called fields or stadiums, but they're all the same thing: a place to play! Over time, the field itself has gotten smaller, and the area around it has gotten bigger. Some teams even play indoors to help with the heat and humidity!

TRUE/FALSE: Baseball stadiums don't allow fans into the stands until the game starts.

Answer: False! Stadiums typically let people come in to see the players warm up and take batting practice.

STELLAR STAT:
In 2019, over 68 million fans attended MAJOR LEAGUE baseball games.

Q&A: What's the oldest baseball stadium in the Major League?

Answer: Fenway Park in Boston. It was opened in 1912, and a lot of it is still unchanged.

STELLAR STAT:

Even though teams had been playing under lights since the 1930s, Wrigley Field in Chicago didn't install lights until 1988. Until then, the CHICAGO CUBS only played day games at home!

GUESTS 05 — INN 04 — HOME 12

BALL 3 — STRIKE 2 — OUT 0

WHO SAID IT?: "I'D GIVE A YEAR OF MY LIFE IF I COULD HIT A HOME RUN ON OPENING DAY OF THIS GREAT NEW PARK."
—BABE RUTH, TALKING ABOUT THE NEW YANKEE STADIUM

TRUE/FALSE: The National Anthem is played before every official game.

Answer: True! It's a tradition that goes back to the 1918 World Series.

"TAKE ME OUT TO THE BALL GAME"

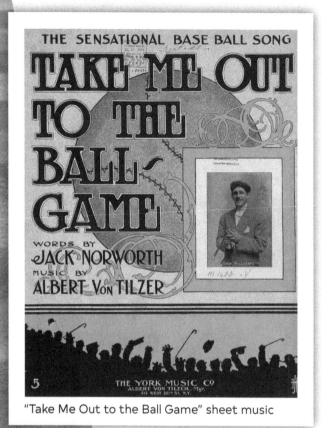

"Take Me Out to the Ball Game" sheet music

Even if you've never been to a game, you've probably heard this song before. It is usually played after the top of the seventh inning, a time of the game called the "stretch," when people get up and stretch their legs. Typically, everyone at the ballpark will sing along and cheer as a way to pep up the home team.

STELLAR STAT: The first instance of the song being played at a MAJOR LEAGUE game was in 1934, during the WORLD SERIES.

TRUE/FALSE: Fans usually sing the entire song during the seventh-inning stretch.

Answer: False! There are actually two verses to the song, and fans only sing the first.

TRUE/FALSE: The writers of the song, Norworth and Von Tilzer, had never been to a Major League baseball game when they wrote the song.

Answer: True! They didn't attend their first Major League game until more than 20 years later!

WHO SAID IT?: "...FOR IT'S ONE, TWO, THREE STRIKES YOU'RE OUT AT THE OLD BALL GAME!"
—"TAKE ME OUT TO THE BALL GAME," BY JACK NORWORTH AND ALBERT VON TILZER

Q&A: When was the song written?

Answer: It was written in 1908 by Jack Norworth and Albert Von Tilzer. Norworth was inspired when he saw a sign for a New York Giants game from his morning train.

STELLAR STAT: Oftentimes, the line "ROOT ROOT ROOT FOR THE HOME TEAM" is replaced with whatever the home team's name is.

PITCHING SPEEDSTERS

Randy Johnson of the Seattle Mariners in 1995

The job of the pitcher has always been to get the batter to strike out. Sometimes the best way to do that is to throw very fast. Over the years, pitchers have figured out how to throw the ball faster and faster; it's amazing the batters can even keep up.

Q&A: How do they figure out the pitch speed?

Answer: Cameras mounted in three places across the field measure the speed and spin of every pitch. Before 2006, teams used radar guns from the upper levels of the field.

TRUE/FALSE: Before the Live Ball Era, which began in 1920, pitchers didn't throw very hard.

Answer: False! In 1917, Washington Senators pitcher Walter Johnson had his speed measured at as much as 91 miles per hour.

STELLAR STAT: The fastest recorded pitch ever thrown was made by AROLDIS CHAPMAN in 2010. It measured a blazing 105.1 miles per hour.

TRUE/FALSE: The average speed of a fastball in today's game is 93 miles per hour.

Answer: True! 93.4 miles per hour.

WHO SAID IT?: "THE GOOD RISING FASTBALL IS THE BEST PITCH IN BASEBALL." —HALL OF FAME PITCHER TOM SEAVER

Q&A: Who was the best fastball pitcher of all time?

Answer: Many say it was Nolan Ryan. Ryan struck out 5,714 batters and was the first pitcher to ever have his fastball measured at over 100 miles per hour.

BALLPARK FOOD

Classic ballpark snacks

There's nothing quite like a hot dog at the ballpark. It's the same hot dog as you would have anywhere else, but it's just special when you're watching baseball with it. Now, ballparks offer a lot of different kinds of food for hungry fans who want to enjoy a game.

Q&A: What other types of food are at ballparks?

Answer: Chicken fingers, cheeseburgers, nachos, and pretzels are all good examples. Usually, each ballpark has its own signature dish.

STELLAR STAT: Cracker Jack made its debut at the FIRST WORLD'S FAIR in 1893. When it got a spot in the chorus of "Take Me Out to the Ball Game," it became a ballpark favorite!

TRUE/FALSE: Hot dogs were first sold at ballparks in the 1920s.

Answer: False! No one actually knows the history behind when they started being sold at ballparks, but many guess it was in the late 1800s.

STELLAR STAT:

On average, Americans eat over 600 million pounds of PEANUTS PER YEAR, a lot of them at baseball games!

TRUE/FALSE: Babe Ruth once ate 12 hot dogs and drank eight bottles of soda at a game.

Answer: True! He had to be rushed to the hospital with indigestion. The incident was called "the belly ache heard 'round the world."

WHO SAID IT?: "WHEN WE WIN... I EAT A LOT. WHEN WE LOSE... I EAT A LOT. WHEN WE'RE RAINED OUT... I EAT A LOT."
—HALL OF FAME MANAGER TOMMY LASORDA

THE HALL OF FAME

Joe DiMaggio of the New York Yankees at the Hall of Fame in 1955

Cooperstown, New York, is a pretty small town. It has some hotels and diners. And the National Baseball Hall of Fame and Museum. Once a year, baseball fans, writers, players, and team owners gather in this small town to honor the best players of their time who are getting their space in the Hall of Fame.

STELLAR STAT: The FIRST PLAYERS elected to the Hall in 1936 were Babe Ruth, Ty Cobb, Honus Wagner, Walter Johnson, and Christy Mathewson.

Q&A: How do they pick who gets in?

Answer: After a player has played for 10 seasons and has been retired for five seasons after that, he is eligible to be voted in. Then the Baseball Writers' Association of America (BBWAA) picks 10 names from a list of players. Any player who gets at least 75 percent of the vote gets in.

Q&A: What if a player doesn't get enough votes?

Answer: Then they stay on the list for next year, until after 10 years. Then they drop off and can't be voted in.

STELLAR STAT: CONNIE MACK **(page 16) and** JOHN MCGRAW **were the first managers ever elected to the Hall of Fame.**

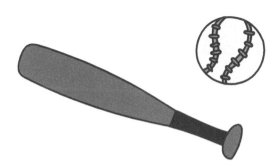

WHO SAID IT?: "SO I'M UGLY, SO WHAT? I NEVER SAW ANYONE HIT WITH HIS FACE." —HALL OF FAME CATCHER YOGI BERRA

TRUE/FALSE: Members of the Hall of Fame are elected by players.

Answer: False! An association of writers called the Baseball Writers' Association of America (BBWAA) elects the members every year.

TALKING THE TALK: JARGON EVERY YOUNG FAN SHOULD KNOW

Baseball has its own language sometimes. There are certain words or phrases that many people use in the game that mean something completely different everywhere else. Some don't really make a lot of sense. Here are a few key words and phrases to remember.

IN THE FIELD

CAN OF CORN: A high fly ball that's easy to catch

DOUBLE PLAY: When the fielders get two outs on the same play

LAYING OUT: When a fielder dives to catch a ball

An outfielder "laying out" to make a catch

ON THE MOUND

1-2-3 INNING: When the pitcher gets three outs in a row to end the inning

CAUGHT LOOKING: When a pitcher gets a strike without the batter swinging at it

FREE PASS: When the batter gets four balls and takes a walk to first base

OTHER FUN NAMES FOR HOME RUNS

FOUR BAGGER

BIG FLY

DINGER

ROUND TRIPPER

PLACES IN THE PARK

BULLPEN: Where the pitchers warm up before coming into the game

THE BLEACHERS: Often referring to the outfield seats

FOUL TERRITORY: The area outside the fair lines

RESOURCES

Baseball Almanac (www.baseball-almanac.com): Over 500,000 pages of baseball history, including game results, records, and even a list of the oldest living baseball players.

Baseball Hall of Fame (www.baseballhall.org): Official website of the Baseball Hall of Fame. Take a look at tours and events; they still hold the induction ceremonies at the Hall every year!

Boys & Girls Clubs of America (www.bgca.org/programs/sports -recreation): Want to play ball? See if there's a league or club in your area.

Major League Baseball official website (www.mlb.com): Follow all of the latest news on your favorite teams.

Minor League Baseball official site (www.milb.com): Official site for Minor League baseball. Minor League games are great ways to see players in a smaller environment. Chances are there's an MiLB team near you.

Baseball Reference (www.baseball-reference.com): Great source for looking up statistics and record holders.

FanSided Network (www.fansided.com/mlb): A network of webpages for all of your favorite teams, written by fans just like you!

Your local library: Your local library has tons of books on the history of baseball, how to play, and more.

GLOSSARY

All-Star: Every year, the fans and players vote on the best players for the first half of the season for the National and American Leagues. Those players get to play in the All-Star Game. To be voted onto the team is considered an honor.

batting average: The percentage of the time that a batter gets a hit when he come up to bat. For example, if he gets a hit 33 out of 100 times, he has a .333 batting average.

Hall of Fame: A museum in Cooperstown, New York, where the greatest players in the history of the game are remembered.

home run: When the batter is able to hit the ball and make it all the way around the bases to home plate. Usually the baseball leaves the field of play (goes over the fence). But it can happen if the defense can't get the ball in time, too.

inning: A part of a baseball game when each team takes a turn at bat. The team that's playing at the other team's field bats first, and then the home team bats second. Each game has nine innings per game. If the score is tied after nine innings, then the teams play extra innings.

manager: Another word for coach. He (or she) is in charge of the team while the players are on the field and decides on the batting order, pitchers, and more.

MVP: Short for Most Valuable Player award, given every year to the player deemed the most valuable in the league.

out: When a batter makes an out, that means that the pitcher or the opposing defense prevented him from getting on base. After three outs, the team that was in the field gets a chance to bat, and the team at bat takes the field.

pennant: When a team wins their league, it's called "winning the pennant," since that team gets a pennant to hang in their stadium forever!

run: When a base runner makes it to home plate safely, the score is called a run. The team with the most runs at the end of the game is the winner.

runs batted in: When a runner scores, the batter that hit the ball to get them home is given credit for that run.

steal: When a base runner advances to the next base without the batter needing to get a hit. Usually the catcher is responsible for throwing runners out when they try to steal.

strikeout: When a pitcher is able to get three pitches in the strike zone past the batter. The batter either swings and misses or doesn't swing and the ball is in the strike zone. Then the batter is out.

walk: When a batter gets to take first base because he doesn't swing at four pitches that are outside the strike zone.

INDEX

ABOUT THE AUTHOR

Adam C. MacKinnon is a contributing baseball writer for Baseball Almanac and Call to the Pen and the founder of *Romantic About Baseball*, a baseball blog. He has been a baseball fan all his life and has followed the Atlanta Braves just as long. He currently resides in Powder Springs, Georgia, with his wife and daughter.

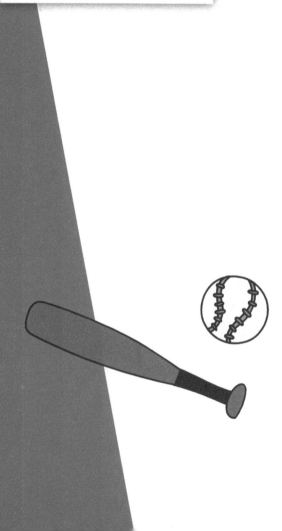

Copyright © 2020 by Rockridge Press, Emeryville, California

No part of this publication may be reproduced, stored in a retrieval system, or transmitted in any form or by any means, electronic, mechanical, photocopying, recording, scanning, or otherwise, except as permitted under Sections 107 or 108 of the 1976 United States Copyright Act, without the prior written permission of the Publisher. Requests to the Publisher for permission should be addressed to the Permissions Department, Rockridge Press, 6005 Shellmound Street, Suite 175, Emeryville, CA 94608.

Limit of Liability/Disclaimer of Warranty: The Publisher and the author make no representations or warranties with respect to the accuracy or completeness of the contents of this work and specifically disclaim all warranties, including without limitation warranties of fitness for a particular purpose. No warranty may be created or extended by sales or promotional materials. The advice and strategies contained herein may not be suitable for every situation. This work is sold with the understanding that the Publisher is not engaged in rendering medical, legal, or other professional advice or services. If professional assistance is required, the services of a competent professional person should be sought. Neither the Publisher nor the author shall be liable for damages arising herefrom. The fact that an individual, organization, or website is referred to in this work as a citation and/or potential source of further information does not mean that the author or the Publisher endorses the information the individual, organization, or website may provide or recommendations they/it may make. Further, readers should be aware that websites listed in this work may have changed or disappeared between when this work was written and when it is read.

For general information on our other products and services or to obtain technical support, please contact our Customer Care Department within the United States at (866) 744-2665, or outside the United States at (510) 253-0500.

Rockridge Press publishes its books in a variety of electronic and print formats. Some content that appears in print may not be available in electronic books, and vice versa.

TRADEMARKS: Rockridge Press and the Rockridge Press logo are trademarks or registered trademarks of Callisto Media Inc. and/or its affiliates, in the United States and other countries, and may not be used without written permission. All other trademarks are the property of their respective owners. Rockridge Press is not associated with any product or vendor mentioned in this book.

Interior and Cover Designer: Stephanie Sumulong
Art Producer: Sue Bischofberger
Editor: Barbara J. Isenberg
Production Editor: Mia Moran

Photography courtesy of Library of Congress/reproduction number LC-USZC4-6147, cover; George Grantham Bain Collection/Library of Congress/reproduction number LC-DIG-ppmsca-18467, cover and p. 6; George Grantham Bain Collection/Library of Congress/reproduction number LC-DIG-ggbain-13809, cover and p. 7; George Grantham Bain Collection/Library of Congress/reproduction number LC-USZ62-97873 DLC, cover and p. 8; Biographical File series/Library of Congress/reproduction number LC-USZ62-105246, cover and p. 11; George Grantham Bain Collection/Library of Congress/reproduction number LC-DIG-ggbain-17514, cover and p. 16; Harris & Ewing/Library of Congress/reproduction number LC-DIG-hec-22989, cover and p. 52; Carol M. Highsmith Archive/Library of Congress/reproduction number LC-DIG-highsm-58461, cover and p. 62; The New York Music Co./Music Division/Library of Congress, https://www.loc.gov/item/ihas.200033481/, cover and p. 64; imkruger/iStock, pp. 1, 25, and 49; Bettman via Getty Images, pp. 2, 5, 27, 28, 37, and 72; National Baseball Hall of Fame Library/MLB via Getty Images, pp. 3, 12, 13, and 40; George Grantham Bain Collection/Library of Congress/reproduction number LC-USZ62-91940, p. 4; lutherhill/iStock, pp. 9 and 33; Peter Newark American Pictures/Bridgeman Images, p. 10; MPI/Getty Images, p. 14; George Rinhart/Corbis via Getty Images, p. 15; Chris Hayward/iStock, pp. 17 and 41; Sporting News via Getty Images, p. 18; Mark Rucker/Transcendental Graphics/Getty Images, p. 19; Minnesota Historical Society/Corbis via Getty Images, p. 20; Library of Congress/reproduction number LC-DIG-ppmsca-18794, p. 21; Mark Rucker/Transcendental Graphics/Getty Images, p. 22; Photo File/MLB Photos via Getty Images, p. 23; RLFE Pix/Alamy Stock Photo, pp. 24, 32, 35, and 56; Antiqua Print Gallery/Alamy Stock Photo, p. 26; Volodymyr Maksymchuk/Alamy Stock Photo, p. 29; Richard Meek/Sports Illustrated via Getty Images, p. 30; Ken Hawkins/Alamy Stock Photo, p. 31; Diamond Images/Getty Images, p. 34; Paul DeMaria/NY Daily News Archive via Getty Images, p. 36; Focus on Sport/Getty Images, pp. 38 and 42; Sandra Foyt/Alamy Stock Photo, p. 39; 2000 SPX/Diamond Images via Getty Images, p. 43; Elsa/Getty Images, p. 44; Brian Lanker/Sports Illustrated via Getty Images, p. 45; patty_c/iStock, p. 46; PCN Photography/Alamy Stock Photo, p. 47; Rob Carr/Getty Images, p. 48; Bruce Leighty Sports Images/Alamy Stock Photo, p. 50; YAY Media AS/Alamy Stock Photo, p. 54; Walter Iooss Jr./Sports Illustrated via Getty Images, p. 58; Martin Mills/Getty Images, p. 60; John Iacono/Sports Illustrated via Getty Images, p. 66; Arina P Habich/shutterstock, p. 68; Cliff Welch/Icon Sportswire via Getty Images, p. 70

Illustration courtesy of Vectorstockersland/Creative Market

ISBN: Print 978-1-64611-237-1 | eBook 978-1-64611-238-8

R0

CPSIA information can be obtained
at www.ICGtesting.com
Printed in the USA
JSHW051504250921
18978JS00001B/3